Parenting with Proverbs

Parenting with Proverbs

LUKE & TRISHA Gilkerson

THE ART OF CORRECTION USING BIBLICAL WISDOM

Parenting with Proverbs:
The Art of Correction Using Biblical Wisdom

By: Luke and Trisha Gilkerson

Intoxicated on Life • Copyright 2015

ISBN-13: 978-1516981786

ISBN-10: 1516981782

Independent publishing services provided by Melinda Martin of TheHelpyHelper.com.

CONTENTS

INTRODUCTION

Brevity is not one of my talents. I am often quick to speak and slow to listen. I use two words where only one will do. Kind people might call me prolific. Honest people might call me a blabber mouth.

The same is true when it comes to correcting my children. In moments of disobedience, defiance, complaining, or arguing, I default to strong words, loud words, or too many words to rein in my kids. In my worst moments, I rely on the strength of my voice, not the strength of what I'm saying, to get the point across.

In His wisdom, God did not leave parents without a lifeline. He inspired a whole book in the Bible specifically for young people, written from a parent's perspective, written to help correct children in the moment-by-moment conversations of the day.

It is the book of Proverbs.

One of the reasons why Solomon and other divinely inspired authors wrote Proverbs was "to give prudence to the simple, knowledge and discretion to the youth" (Prov. 1:4). Nearly 20 times in the introductory chapters of Proverbs, Solomon uses the phrase "my son" or "my children." The heartbeat of the book of Proverbs is intensely personal and fatherly: "My son, give me your heart, and let your eyes observe my ways" (23:26). This is what makes the book ideal for parenting.

Proverbs is a book of parental and stately wisdom designed by God to be taught to the young — the little child to the young adult.

A LITTLE ABOUT PROVERBS

The material in the Book of Proverbs was first written and collected by King Solomon, who is said to have spoken some 3,000 proverbs in his lifetime (1 Kings 4:29-34). Others came along later to compile more proverbial sayings and put the book into its final form.

The key term in the Book of Proverbs is "wisdom." This word (*khokmah* in Hebrew) could be rightly translated "skill"—a skill for choosing the right course of action to get a desired result. You might think of wisdom as "skill in the art of godly living."

The first nine chapters of Proverbs contain lengthly poems: a father's invitation to readers to pursue wisdom. The chapters that follow mostly contain specific proverbs: short, punchy statements that address a specific aspect of living wisely.

5 REASONS PROVERBS ARE IDEAL FOR CORRECTION

Proverbs is like the Twitter of the Bible. I don't mean that with any disrespect. Training your mind to come up with something winsome, compelling, and provocative in only a few words is demanding. Saying something brief and powerful is difficult to do. As Blaise Pascal said, "I would have written a shorter letter, but I did not have the time."

But God has given parents a whole book of pithy, powerful statements.

The book of Proverbs encapsulates quick moral lessons and wise thoughts into short phrases, and this makes them ideal tools for parents to use in correcting children.

1. **PROVERBS ARE SHORT** – When you need to steer a child's behavior in the moment, a short statement is best. A proverb quickly anchors your thoughts on what needs to be corrected.

2. **THEY ARE MEMORABLE AND QUOTABLE** – The Proverbs were written to be memorized and quoted aloud.

3. **PROVERBS STATE THE *WHY*, NOT JUST THE *WHAT*** – Proverbs don't just say, "Stop it!" or "Do this!" They say, "This is wise because…."

4. **THEY ARE BASED ON REAL EXPERIENCE** – Proverbs are "rules of thumb," general truths based on human experiences. They are convincing because they summarize the collective experiences of many people from the past.

5. **THEY ARE GOD'S WORDS** – When you use the Proverbs, rather than pointing merely to your own authority as a parent, you are pointing to God's authority. If your children continue to disobey, they do so knowing they are contending with God, not you.

THE PROVERBS METHOD OF CORRECTION

Below is a simple method for moral training for your children using the proverbs.

STEP #1: MAKE A LIST OF THE MOST PRESSING BEHAVIOR ISSUES YOUR CHILDREN HAVE.

Sit down in a quiet moment (preferably with your spouse if you are married) and think through all the behavior concerns you have for your kids. Pick from the list of proverbs in this book to help you.

STEP #2: PICK THE TOP TWO OR THREE ISSUES.

The aim isn't to correct everything all at once, but to pick the top two or three most pressing issues—the ones that come up more often or seem to be the most life-disturbing for the family.

STEP #3: FIND THE BEST PROVERB FOR EACH ISSUE.

Keep it simple. Choose just one proverb for each issue. Choose the one you think fits your child the best.

STEP #4: COMMIT EACH PROVERB TO MEMORY.

Take time to memorize each proverb you've selected. My preferred method is to "stuff" the Bible passage daily: repeat the verse aloud over and over for 5 minutes a day. Do that for a couple weeks or until you feel you really have the proverb down cold. Set a reminder for yourself to review the verses every few days, then once a week, then once a month—pushing the verses into your long-term memory.

STEP #5: DISCUSS AND APPLY EACH PROVERB.

Whenever is most natural—during family devotions, mealtimes, tucking them in at night, etc.—discuss each proverb with your children. Talk about what each proverb means and how it applies to your lives—not just for your kids, but for you as well.

Lastly, make sure you apply the proverb to the life of Christ. Remember: Jesus is the ultimate Wise Son who perfectly displayed a righteous life. Doing this, we avoid turning the Book of Proverbs into moralistic demands, and we remind our kids that no matter how many times we act foolishly, God's grace is bigger.

STEP #6: START USING EACH PROVERB IN PROBLEM MOMENTS.

After you've discussed the relevant proverb with your children in a calm moment, the next time you see the behavior problem:

1. **PAUSE AND GET CLOSE TO YOUR CHILD** – When we purpose to use proverbs to correct our children, this offers a great corrective to us as parents as well. When you are intentional about dispensing proverbial wisdom, you are forced to stop, think, and collect your whits before you

talk. You are forced to get into a posture of instruction. Let's face it: proverbs sound pretty stupid when you shout them across a chaotic room. So pause, get close to your child, look them in the eye, and get their attention.

2. **LISTEN TO YOUR CHILD'S HEART FIRST** – Don't push the child's emotions aside. Remember: "If one gives an answer before he hears, it is his folly and shame" (Prov. 18:13). It may help to repeat back to your child the emotions or thoughts you think he or she is having at that moment: "You're upset because…" "When you did this you wanted…" "When you acted this way, you were trying to…" This lets your children know you hear their hearts.

3. **REMIND YOUR CHILD WHAT THE PROVERB SAYS** – Start by saying, "Remember what the Scriptures say…" or "Remember what the Proverbs say…" or simply "Remember…" Then quote it aloud. Because you have the proverb memorized, you will sound confident and definite in your stance.

4. **GIVE A SIMPLE INTERPRETATION** – Interpret the proverb in simple terms. Use this basic template: "This means it is wise/good to [behavior/attitude], because if we do [promised blessing]" or "This means it is unwise/bad to [behavior/attitude], because if we do [consequence]."

5. **IF THE TIME IS RIGHT, ENGAGE IN DIALOGUE** – The time may not be right to get into a discussion, or your child may be too young to respond with an intelligent thought. However, if the opportunity is ripe, ask your child to think

about the long-term consequences of their behavior or attitude. How would their life be different if they manifested wiser behavior?

6. **STATE CLEAR EXPECTATIONS** – Once your child has heard you and understood, state your expectations for what he or she should do next.

STEP #7: START USING EACH PROVERB IN MOMENTS OF VIRTUE.

Don't just use the proverb to correct. Use it to encourage good behavior. When your children display moments of virtue, let them know you noticed, quote the proverb, and reinforce the blessing implied by the proverb for their proper behavior.

LATHER, RINSE, REPEAT

Do this for each problem or issue with your children.

In time, your child will start to know some of these proverbs by heart. You'll be able to state the beginning of the proverb and they will be able to respond with the end. The proverbs will start to become a shared language in your home.

CHARACTER TRAITS IN THE PROVERBS

This section presents 14 character qualities. Because Biblical proverbs often contrast evil or unwise qualities with godly or wise qualities, we have paired bad and good character traits together below.

Each pair of qualities has the following to help you:

- A sample proverb.

- An initial Bible study of that proverb: something you can teach your children during family devotions.

- A quick interpretation for correction: a short explanation of what the proverb means that you can use in a moment of correction.

- Dialogue questions: conversation questions you can use if the time is ripe.

- A list of alternate proverbs that can be used.

LAZY VS. HARD-WORKING

BIBLE STUDY:

A profit is something valuable you get for doing work. If you have a job, you get money for doing your work. If you do all your homework for school, you get a grade for completing it. If you build a house, you would have a new house to live in. If you plant something in the ground and take care of it, you will eventually get to eat the fruit from that plant.

"IN ALL TOIL THERE IS PROFIT, BUT MERE TALK TENDS ONLY TO POVERTY." (14:23)

People like the profits from work, but not everyone likes to work hard. Some people talk as if they are going to work, but they never do. They may say, "Tomorrow I'm going to work hard and earn some money," but when tomorrow comes, they don't work. If you don't work, you don't get any profit.

Jesus was a man of action, not just talk. He didn't just tell us that he loves us. He actually got up from his heavenly throne, came to earth as a man, and worked hard his whole life. Read the stories of Jesus' life. During his ministry he was always on the move. He would rise early to pray, serve and teach people all day long, and walk from town to town. One day Jesus was so tired he was able to sleep in the middle of a huge thunder storm. Jesus was a hard worker.

It is a good thing Jesus was a hard worker because one day God the Father had a very hard job for Him to do. It was a plan they had long before Jesus came to earth. Jesus was going to have to die for our sins on the cross. We all deserve death for our sins against God, but Jesus chose to lay down his life for us—to die in our place. This was hard work, but Jesus didn't quit. He didn't just tell us that he loved us. He showed it with action.

What was Jesus' profit for all his hard work? He earned the reward of returning to heaven next to His heavenly Father. God the Father raised Him from the dead and made Jesus the King over the whole universe. Best of all, if we trust Jesus, He shares that profit with us—we can be with Him forever.

We should be a hard-worker just like Jesus was, so we can gain the profit from our hard work.

QUICK INTERPRETATION FOR CORRECTION:

This means it is wise to learn to work hard, because when we do, we receive something valuable in return. People who don't learn to work hard—people who just talk about working—won't end up making the kind of profit they want to make.

DIALOGUE QUESTIONS

1. What kind of profit do you hope to gain by [activity]?

2. What will you lose if you don't work hard at [activity]?

3. Was Jesus a hard worker, or was He lazy?

OTHER PROVERBS

- "A slack hand causes poverty, but the hand of the diligent makes rich." (10:4)

- "Whoever works his land will have plenty of bread, but he who follows worthless pursuits lacks sense." (12:11)

- "The hand of the diligent will rule, while the slothful will be put to forced labor." (12:24)

- "The soul of the sluggard craves and gets nothing, while the soul of the diligent is richly supplied." (13:4)

- "Slothfulness casts into a deep sleep, and an idle person will suffer hunger." (19:15)

- "The desire of the sluggard kills him, for his hands refuse to labor. All day long he craves and craves, but the righteous gives and does not hold back." (21:25-26)

SLOPPY VS. DILIGENT

BIBLE STUDY:

God provides for our needs in many different ways. He sends rain down to water the ground which grows the food we eat. He gives us sunshine to keep us warm and give us light.

> "THE PLANS OF THE DILIGENT LEAD SURELY TO ABUNDANCE, BUT EVERYONE WHO IS HASTY COMES ONLY TO POVERTY." (21:5)

But one of the most important ways God provides for us is by giving us strength to work. He gives us minds to think so we can plan our work. He gives us legs to move us back and forth to our jobs. He gives us hands and mouths so we can labor and conduct business. This work is what allows us to make money and get important tasks done.

There are two kinds of workers. There are those who are diligent: this means they work hard and they work smart. They do good work. They make plans about how to get a job done, and then they follow their plans until the job is complete. Then there are those who are sloppy: this means they only want to take shortcuts and they only care about getting rich quick. They want to rush through their work and don't care about if it is good work.

In the Gospel of Mark, right after Jesus healed a man who was deaf and couldn't talk properly, the people were so amazed they said, "He does all things well" (Mark 7:37). When Jesus served other people, He wasn't sloppy. He healed people all the way, and He was full of compassion.

We must always remember this: Jesus is diligent with us. He isn't absent-minded or distracted. He isn't sloppy. He is at work all around us, shaping us into the kind of people He wants us to be.

We should be diligent workers because a character of diligence will be rewarded.

QUICK INTERPRETATION FOR CORRECTION:

This means if you want to be productive and get the benefits, you have to think through how you can get things done. But if you are always trying to find a shortcut and are sloppy with your work, you won't get what you want.

DIALOGUE QUESTIONS

1. If you slow down and think carefully, what benefit will you get?

2. If you keep rushing through this, what is likely to happen?

3. Was Jesus a diligent worker or a sloppy worker?

OTHER PROVERBS

"Whoever is slack in his work is a brother to him who destroys." (18:9)

"Do you see a man skillful in his work? He will stand before kings; he will not stand before obscure men." (22:29)

"Whoever works his land will have plenty of bread, but he who follows worthless pursuits will have plenty of poverty." (28:19)

"A faithful man will abound with blessings, but whoever hastens to be rich will not go unpunished." (28:20)

DECEITFUL VS. TRUTHFUL

BIBLE STUDY:

"TRUTHFUL LIPS ENDURE FOREVER, BUT A LYING TONGUE IS BUT FOR A MOMENT." (12:19)

The reason why people lie is to get something they want. You may want to avoid getting in trouble, so you lie so people don't find out what you did. You may want to look really good to other people, so you lie about something great you did—but you really didn't do.

The benefits of lying don't last very long, that's why this proverb says a lying tongue is only for a moment. Often people find out about your lie, and then they don't trust you anymore. If you lie over and over again, you get a bad reputation for being a liar and untrustworthy.

In his book, *The Millionaire Mind*, Thomas Stanley surveyed 733 millionaires from around the United States. He asked them a lot of questions about how they got to be so rich and how they spend their money. Do you know what the #1 factor that contributed to their success was? Telling the truth. Because they were truthful people, they have good reputations and were able to be very successful.

Jesus was a man who loved to speak the truth. His disciple Peter later said about Jesus, there was no deceit, no lies, found in his mouth (1 Pet. 2:22). Jesus always spoke the truth. Over 70 times Jesus is recorded saying the phrase "I tell you the truth." In fact, on the day of his trial, right before He was put to death, he told the governor that proclaiming the truth is the very reason why He was born: "For this purpose I was born and for this purpose I have come into the world—to bear witness to the truth" (John 18:37).

Jesus reminds us that truthful lips really do endure forever, just like the proverb says. In fact, after Jesus died, God raise Him from the dead by His mighty power, and Jesus is now in heaven seated on His throne. For all eternity, Jesus will be speaking the truth.

We should always aim to be truthful in everything we say, so we can be known as trustworthy people.

QUICK INTERPRETATION FOR CORRECTION:

This means the benefits of lying don't last very long, but if you are truthful, people are more likely to trust you for the rest of your life.

DIALOGUE QUESTIONS

1. What were you hoping to get by lying?

2. How would telling the truth in that moment have been more beneficial to you?

3. Did Jesus ever need to lie to get something He wanted?

OTHER PROVERBS

"Whoever walks in integrity walks securely, but he who makes his ways crooked will be found out." (10:9)

"Lying lips are an abomination to the Lord, but those who act faithfully are his delight." (12:22)

"A truthful witness saves lives, but one who breathes out lies is deceitful." (14:25)

"A gentle tongue is a tree of life, but perverseness in it breaks the spirit." (15:4)

"Better is a little with righteousness than great revenues with injustice." (16:8)

"A false witness will not go unpunished, and he who breathes out lies will not escape." (19:5)

"A false witness will not go unpunished, and he who breathes out lies will perish." (19:9)

"A lying tongue hates its victims, and a flattering mouth works ruin." (26:28)

EMOTIONALLY IMPULSIVE VS. SELF-CONTROLLED

BIBLE STUDY:

This proverb is a lot like other proverbs in the Bible. It compares two people: the wise person and the fool. One of the things foolish people do is they always say the first thing they feel. If they get angry, they blurt out angry words right away. If something makes them sad, they immediately burst into tears. If something is on their mind, they have to say it right away, and they believe others need to listen right away.

"A FOOL GIVES FULL VENT TO HIS SPIRIT, BUT A WISE MAN QUIETLY HOLDS IT BACK." (12:19)

Now, it is important to remember, God gave us emotions. There's nothing wrong with feeling sad or mad or excited. But a wise person is someone who is learning how not to be controlled by emotions. A wise person is learning how to show his or her emotions at the right time and in the right way.

You might feel upset about something, but instead of immediately crying, you are able to share how you feel without being totally overcome by sadness. You might feel really angry about something, but you are learning to share your anger in a way that doesn't attack people. You might feel really excited to say something, but instead of demanding everyone's attention, you can wait until it is your turn to talk.

Jesus was a man full of emotion. In the Bible we read stories about Jesus being full of compassion, angry, passionate, distressed, sorrowful or grieved, crying, surprised, and leaping for joy. Jesus experienced all kinds of human emotions. But Jesus was never controlled by His emotions.

Think about the time when Jesus was arrested and put on trial. When He was grabbed by the guards, He could have called down thousands of angels to help Him, but He didn't. When He was being accused, He could have spoken up to defend Himself, but He didn't. When people nailed Him to the cross, He could have shouted mean things at them, but He didn't. When people teased Him as He hung on the cross, He could have condemned them all, but He didn't. At the most emotional time of His life, Jesus didn't vent every emotion He had. That's because He wasn't controlled by His emotions.

Because of this, Jesus was the perfect sacrifice on the cross. He never sinned by venting His emotions the wrong way. Because He was perfect, His death on the cross means we can be forgiven for every sin.

We should learn not to be controlled by our emotions, but to hold our emotions back for the appropriate time.

QUICK INTERPRETATION FOR CORRECTION:

This means a wise person is learning to control his or her emotions, but a foolish person feels like they need to burst out with emotion the moment they feel something.

DIALOGUE QUESTIONS

1. Are you in control of your emotions right now, or are they controlling you?

2. When you feel this way, what would be a good way to express your thoughts?

3. Was Jesus controlled by His emotions?

OTHER PROVERBS

"Whoever is slow to anger has great understanding, but he who has a hasty temper exalts folly." (14:29)

"Whoever restrains his words has knowledge, and he who has a cool spirit is a man of understanding." (17:27)

"Whoever keeps his mouth and his tongue keeps himself out of trouble." (21:23)

"With patience a ruler may be persuaded, and a soft tongue will break a bone." (25:15)

"A man without self-control is like a city broken into and left without walls." (25:28)

"Do you see a man who is hasty in his words? There is more hope for a fool than for him." (29:20)

GREEDY VS. GENEROUS

BIBLE STUDY:

This proverb sounds a little mysterious. It's saying this: the more you give, the more you have. How can that be true? If I have ten toys and I give away all ten, I don't have any toys left, so how could I be getting richer?

> "ONE GIVES FREELY, YET GROWS ALL THE RICHER; ANOTHER WITHHOLDS WHAT HE SHOULD GIVE, AND ONLY SUFFERS WANT."
> (11:24)

But the secret to this proverb is God. When we share what we have with others, God blesses us. God can bless us in many different ways, but when we are thinking about the needs and desires of others, God will take care of us.

There are others who are greedy. They don't share with others. They don't give money to those who are poor or in need. They hold everything for themselves. When people are greedy, often they find they are never satisfied. For some, they just never have enough.

The Bible says Jesus was the most generous person who ever lived. "Generous" means he didn't just hold onto everything he had—he gave what he had to help others. The Bible says, "For you know the grace of our Lord Jesus Christ, that though he was rich, yet for your sake he became poor, so that you by his poverty might become rich" (2 Cor. 8:9).

Before He became a man and came to earth, Jesus was the richest person in the universe. He was the Prince of heaven. He never experienced hunger, pain, or sickness. Then He became a human being and lived in a poor family. He was surrounded by sickness, pain, and hunger. He gave His time to help people, heal them, teach them, and be friends with them.

Finally, at the end of His life, He gave away everything He had: He gave His life on the cross so we could be forgiven for all our sins. Now, because of what He gave, we can be with God forever—we get to have all the riches of heaven. Jesus made Himself poor so we could become rich.

And just like this proverb says: Jesus gave freely but still got richer. God took care of all Jesus' needs throughout His life, and then after Jesus died, God raised Him from the dead. Now, Jesus is at the right hand of God the Father in heaven again. He is the richest person in the universe.

This is how we should be as well. If we see somebody needs or wants something, we should be thinking about this proverb: give freely and trust God. God loves a cheerful giver.

QUICK INTERPRETATION FOR CORRECTION:

This means it is wise to give—be generous—to others because God will take care of our needs, but if we are greedy, it never feels like we have enough.

DIALOGUE QUESTIONS

1. Are you being generous right now, or are you being greedy?

2. When you are greedy, how does it make you feel?

3. Was Jesus greedy or generous?

OTHER PROVERBS

"Whoever brings blessing will be enriched, and one who waters will himself be watered." (11:25)

"Whoever despises his neighbor is a sinner, but blessed is he who is generous to the poor." (14:21)

"Whoever oppresses a poor man insults his Maker, but he who is generous to the needy honors him." (14:31)

"Whoever is generous to the poor lends to the Lord, and he will repay him for his deed." (19:17)

"Whoever closes his ear to the cry of the poor will himself call out and not be answered." (21:13)

"Whoever has a bountiful eye will be blessed, for he shares his bread with the poor." (22:9)

"A greedy man stirs up strife, but the one who trusts in the Lord will be enriched. (28:25)

"Whoever gives to the poor will not want, but he who hides his eyes will get many a curse. (28:27)

INDIFFERENT VS. ATTENTIVE TO ELDERS

BIBLE STUDY:

This proverb says there are two ways you can go: you can be wise or you can be foolish. A foolish person only listens to their own advice. They have an idea in their mind, and they love that idea so much they don't want to listen to anyone else. They don't want to listen to people who might be older or wiser or people have more experience. They don't want to listen to people who have different ideas. They just want to do what they want to do.

"THE WAY OF A FOOL IS RIGHT IN HIS OWN EYES, BUT A WISE MAN LISTENS TO ADVICE." (12:15)

The wise person listens to advice. They may not always follow the advice, but they at least listen. They don't think, "I know what to do. I don't need any help." They think, "I need other people to help me understand what is best."

Even though Jesus was the Son of God, He listened. When He was a young boy, His parents found Him in the temple, sitting among the teachers and asking them questions (Luke 2:46). The Bible says throughout his childhood, he grew in wisdom (2:52). Even when He was a grown up,

Jesus still needed the wisdom of His heavenly Father. He said, "I can do nothing on my own. As I hear, I judge, and my judgment is just, because I seek not my own will but the will of him who sent me" (John 5:30). He said even though He was the perfect Son of God, He still needed to hear from His Father in heaven in order to make the right decisions.

This is how we should be as well. When I give you advice about how to do something, it is important for you to listen. When other older people give you advice, it is important that you listen. This proverb is about your attitude: even if you don't follow my advice, your attitude should be, "I need help understanding. I am glad to listen, so I can learn."

QUICK INTERPRETATION FOR CORRECTION:

This means it is wise to listen when someone gives you advice, but it is foolish to think you know everything.

DIALOGUE QUESTIONS

1. Are you listening right now, or are you just doing things your own way?

2. What might happen to you if you keep living like you know everything?

3. Did Jesus listen to the wisdom of His Father, or was He a know-it-all?

OTHER PROVERBS

"Whoever heeds instruction is on the path to life, but he who rejects reproof leads others astray." (10:17)

"Poverty and disgrace come to him who ignores instruction, but whoever heeds reproof is honored." (13:18)

"Cease to hear instruction, my son, and you will stray from the words of knowledge." (19:27)

ARGUMENTATIVE VS. OBEDIENT

BIBLE STUDY:

It is hard to listen when you're told you are wrong or that you did something wrong. In the Bible, this is called "rebuke," when someone corrects you. It is hard to listen to rebuke because we don't like to be told we are wrong.

> "A WISE SON HEARS HIS FATHER'S INSTRUCTION, BUT A SCOFFER DOES NOT LISTEN TO REBUKE." (13:1)

Those who don't listen to rebuke are called "scoffers." When someone corrects them, they talk back. They think, "I don't have to listen to this person," and they argue back at that person.

But the opposite of a scoffer is someone who is wise. A wise person listens to what their parents have to say. God gave us parents because He wants us to learn, and sometimes learning you have done something wrong can feel bad. That's okay. As we are corrected, we grow into wise people.

Jesus also had to learn from His parents. There's a story in the Bible when Jesus was on a trip with His family to Jerusalem. When it was time to leave, His parents thought Jesus was with their big traveling group, but He wasn't. His parents went back to Jerusalem to find Him. He had been lost for three days when they finally found Him in the temple, talking with the elders of the people.

His parents had been worried about Him, and they were relieved when they found Him, but they were also a little upset. Why had Jesus wandered off? Jesus hadn't done anything wrong, of course, but He could see how much His parents were upset, so the Bible says Jesus went with them back to their hometown "and was submissive to them" (Luke 2:51). He listened to their instruction. He obeyed them. Even though He was the Son of God, He honored His parents.

This is good because in order for Jesus to be the perfect sacrifice for our sins on the cross, this meant He needed to obey God in every way. This includes Jesus honoring His parents. He honored them and listened to them, and because Jesus never scoffed at His parents, never talked back, and because He continued to perfectly obey God throughout His life, He could be the perfect sacrifice for our sins. This is why we can be forgiven for everything we've ever done wrong.

We should be like this as well: we should always honor our parents, listen carefully to them, and never talk back to them. If we do this, the Proverbs say, we will show that we are wise.

QUICK INTERPRETATION FOR CORRECTION:

This means a wise person listens when parents correct them, but a foolish person doesn't care what parents say and just talks back.

DIALOGUE QUESTIONS

1. Were you really listening to me when I corrected you, or were you talking back?

2. Why is someone who scoffs at his parents foolish?

3. Did Jesus scoff at His parents, or did He listen to them?

OTHER PROVERBS

"Whoever loves discipline loves knowledge, but he who hates reproof is stupid." (12:1)

"By insolence comes nothing but strife, but with those who take advice is wisdom." (13:10)

"A fool despises his father's instruction, but whoever heeds reproof is prudent." (15:5)

"He who is often reproved, yet stiffens his neck, will suddenly be broken beyond healing." (29:1)

HURTFUL WORDS VS. KIND WORDS

BIBLE STUDY:

When people disagree, often it is easy to get angry. Throughout your whole life, you'll be tempted to get angry at others, and people will get angry around you. The most important thing we can do is remember how to react when others are angry.

"A SOFT ANSWER TURNS AWAY WRATH, BUT A HARSH WORD STIRS UP ANGER." (15:1)

This proverb says if someone is getting mad around you, the best way to help them calm down is to be calm yourself. If someone shouts at you, shouting back won't help them calm down. If someone calls you a name, don't call them a name back. When someone gets mad at you, don't get mad back at them. When you see others getting upset or frustrated, the best way to react is to be gentle.

Jesus understood this as well. Once Jesus was sitting in the temple teaching the people. The religious leaders brought in a woman who had just been found guilty of doing something really bad. According to the law, she should be punished—they were going to kill her because of her crime. The crowds were there getting very upset, picking up rocks getting ready to throw them at her. The religious teachers asked Jesus, "What should we do to her?"

Jesus didn't get upset. He didn't get mad. He didn't start shouting. Instead he knelt down and started writing in the dirt. Now, the Bible doesn't tell us what He wrote. It really doesn't matter what He wrote. He was pausing before He said anything. He was thinking. He was showing them, "I'm not just going to react to your anger right now. I'm not going to get upset just because you're upset."

Then, he silenced the angry crowds with one calm statement: "Let him who is without sin among you be the first to throw a stone at her" (John 8:7). He was saying, "You want to kill her? Okay. Anyone here who isn't guilty of sin should be the first to throw a stone." Then he bent over and started writing in the dirt again.

One by one, people threw down their rocks and walked away. Everyone there started thinking of their own sins, they calmed down, and they walked away. Finally, no one was there except Jesus and the woman. Jesus' calm reaction and wise words had calmed the angry crowds.

We should be like this as well. When others get upset, instead of reacting with anger or loud words, we should pause, make sure we are calm, and then speak with gentle words in a gentle tone of voice.

QUICK INTERPRETATION FOR CORRECTION:

This means if we want to create a more peaceful situation, it is important to respond in a calm way and with wise words.

DIALOGUE QUESTIONS

1. Are you speaking in a calm way right now or were you being harsh?

2. When someone else is upset, how can we remember to stay calm?

3. When people were angry at Jesus, did He just react in anger, or did He think before He spoke?

OTHER PROVERBS

"Whoever belittles his neighbor lacks sense, but a man of understanding remains silent." (11:12)

"A man who is kind benefits himself, but a cruel man hurts himself." (11:17)

"There is one whose rash words are like sword thrusts, but the tongue of the wise brings healing." (12:18)

"Gracious words are like a honeycomb, sweetness to the soul and health to the body." (16:24)

"He who loves purity of heart, and whose speech is gracious, will have the king as his friend." (22:11)

PRIDEFUL VS. HUMBLE

BIBLE STUDY:

Do you know what the word "pride" means? When you act like you are more important than other people or better than other people, it means you are prideful. When you are prideful, you might brag about what you've done, hoping others will think you are great. When you are prideful, you might be really selfish, always trying to get first in line or get the best toys.

> "ONE'S PRIDE WILL BRING HIM LOW, BUT HE WHO IS LOWLY IN SPIRIT WILL OBTAIN HONOR." (12:15)

Instead, we should be humble. When this proverb is talking about being lowly in spirit, it means you put others before yourself. It means you act like a servant to others. You treat others as more important than yourself.

We do this because we know where real honor comes from. It comes from God. God honors those who bring themselves low and serve others. When you are prideful, neither God nor other people will honor you, because you are only caring about yourself.

Jesus said something similar when He was on Earth: "For everyone who exalts himself will be humbled, and he who humbles himself will be exalted" (Luke 14:11). And Jesus lived this way, as well. One evening when He was eating with His disciples, He got up, wrapped a towel around His waist, and He washed His disciples' feet the way a servant might do. Imagine how surprised His disciples were: here was their teacher, the man they called Lord, washing their feet, the lowest kind of job a person could have. He said to them, "I have given you an example, that you also should do just as I have done to you" (John 13:15). If our Lord was willing to act like a servant, we should be willing to serve others.

Jesus humbled Himself all through His life. He humbled Himself when He emptied Himself and became a human being (Phil. 2:7) while He lived on Earth. But the most humbling thing He did is when He obeyed His heavenly Father and died on a cross. Nothing could have been more humiliating and painful than dying like that. But He did it, not just to obey the Father, but to serve us. Because He paid the price for our sins, we can be with God forever.

Just as this proverb says, the one who is lowly in spirit will obtain honor: the Father honored Jesus after He died by raising Him from the dead and seating Jesus at the place of greatest honor in heaven. The Father gave Him a name that is above every name: "Lord." Some day every knee will bow to Jesus and every tongue confess that He is Lord (Phil. 2:9-11).

We should be lowly like Jesus as well. If we are humble, put others first, in time God will honor us, possibly in this life, and definitely in the life to come.

QUICK INTERPRETATION FOR CORRECTION:

This means if we always want to be first or most important, the honor we get won't last, but if we serve others, God will honor us.

DIALOGUE QUESTIONS

1. Were you being prideful just now or humble?

2. How do you think God honors those who are servant-hearted?

3. In what ways was Jesus humble?

OTHER PROVERBS

"Everyone who is arrogant in heart is an abomination to the Lord; be assured, he will not go unpunished." (16:5)

"It is not good to eat much honey, nor is it glorious to seek one's own glory." (25:27)

"Let another praise you, and not your own mouth; a stranger, and not your own lips." (27:2)

ENVIOUS VS. REJOICING WITH OTHERS

BIBLE STUDY:

Envy is a terribly feeling. Do you know what envy is? It is that feeling of wanting to have what someone else has or that feeling of wanting to be what someone else is. You might feel envy if someone has a special new toy that you want or if someone got to go somewhere special or someone has more money than you or someone has a job you want. You can feel envy about anything, and it usually makes you really sad because you start thinking about all the stuff you want that you don't have. That's why this proverb says envy rots the bones: it wears you out and makes you feel awful.

> "A TRANQUIL HEART GIVES LIFE TO THE FLESH, BUT ENVY MAKES THE BONES ROT." (14:30)

Instead we should have a calm heart. It is okay to want something, but a calm heart won't get carried away. We should be happy for others when they have nice things, when they are blessed, instead of being upset that we don't have what they have. We should be content with what we have. If we do, the Bible says we will actually feel better and be healthier.

Even modern medicine agrees with this: people who feel more content, joyful, and kind to others are healthier people.

Jesus had a perfectly calm and tranquil heart. First, He wasn't obsessed with getting more material things in life. He wasn't obsessed with money or what money could buy. Jesus said, "One's life does not consist in the abundance of his possessions" (Luke 12:15), meaning that life is not about getting more things. Jesus didn't care how much he owned. He only cared if He did what His Father wanted Him to do.

Jesus also had a tranquil and calm heart because He wasn't focused just on the things going on right now; He was focused on eternal things. Jesus was always talking about the kingdom of God, talking about the day He returned to earth and would change the whole world. All the riches we get in this life can't possibly compare to the riches of the new world that is to come.

This is why Jesus never felt envy. He knew the stuff money could buy was only temporary, but the blessings of eternal life are forever.

We should follow in Jesus' footsteps. Any time we see someone with something we want, instead of immediately feeling jealous, we should be happy for them and remind ourselves: "Life isn't about getting more things. It's about being loved by and loving God."

QUICK INTERPRETATION FOR CORRECTION:

This means envy only makes us feel bad, but we feel much better in life if we are happy for others.

DIALOGUE QUESTIONS

1. Were you acting envious just now, or were you happy for someone else?

2. If you felt envious all the time, do you think you would feel happy?

3. Was Jesus ever envious, or was His focus on other things?

OTHER PROVERBS

"The righteous has enough to satisfy his appetite, but the belly of the wicked suffers want." (13:25)

"Let not your heart envy sinners, but continue in the fear of the Lord all the day." (23:17)

"Be not envious of evil men, nor desire to be with them, for their hearts devise violence, and their lips talk of trouble." (24:1-2)

"Fret not yourself because of evildoers, and be not envious of the wicked, for the evil man has no future; the lamp of the wicked will be put out." (24:19-20)

QUARRELING VS. PEACEMAKING

BIBLE STUDY:

It's normal for people to disagree. We all have different opinions. We all want different things. This means people sometimes get into contentions or fights. The key is how we should react. We can either try to quiet the fight, or we can stir it up and make it worse.

"A HOT-TEMPERED MAN STIRS UP STRIVE, BUT HE WHO IS SLOW TO ANGER QUIETS CONTENTION." (15:18)

We make it worse if we are hot-tempered. This means we just burst out with our own thoughts. We get angry or upset easily. If we are like that, we aren't being a peacemaker. We are just getting ourselves and everybody else more upset.

But we can be a peacemaker if we are slow to anger. Notice, this proverb doesn't say we should never get angry. Anger isn't always a bad thing. Even God gets angry, but He always gets angry about the right things, in the right way, for the right reason, and is never out of control with His anger. We should try to be the same way. We shouldn't get angry just because we are annoyed at someone. We shouldn't get angry in a way that attacks people and cuts them down. We should never just blow up in anger. We should be very slow to anger.

If we are slow to anger, it will also help to quiet fights when people disagree. This is what it means to be a peacemaker: we help to calm down disagreements and fights.

Jesus, as the Son of God, is the greatest peacemaker ever. Numerous times we read how the disciples got into fights about which one was the greatest disciple. Each time, Jesus was slow to anger and gently corrected them (Luke 9:46-48; 22:24-27).

Jesus will also bring peace to the whole world. In the world, there are many nations that war against each other. But as more people become Christians, they are no longer enemies, but brothers and sisters in Christ. The Bible says we are no longer outsiders, but we are "fellow citizens with the saints and members of the household of God" (Eph. 2:19). Because of Jesus' death on the cross, we can come near to God and therefore near to each other in peace. When Jesus returns, the world will be a place of perfect peace. Everyone will worship the same God and "nation shall not lift up sword against nation, neither shall they learn war anymore" (Is. 2:4).

We should try as best we can to be peacemakers like Jesus was. This means we need to be slow to anger so we don't stir up arguments.

QUICK INTERPRETATION FOR CORRECTION:

This means we can be peacemakers by being calm and slow to anger.

DIALOGUE QUESTIONS

1. Were you being a peacemaker or were you stirring up strife?

2. Why is being hot-tempered a bad way to settle arguments?

3. Was Jesus a peacemaker or did he stir up arguments?

OTHER PROVERBS

"The vexation of a fool is known at once, but the prudent ignores an insult." (12:16)

"It is an honor for a man to keep aloof from strife, but every fool will be quarreling." (20:3)

"As charcoal to hot embers and wood to fire, so is a quarrelsome man for kindling strife." (26:21)

"For pressing milk produces curds, pressing the nose produces blood, and pressing anger produces strife." (30:33)

BAD FRIENDSHIPS VS. GOOD RELATIONSHIPS

BIBLE STUDY:

There are different kinds of friends we can have in our lives. We can have friends who are foolish, or we can have friends who are wise. If we hang out with foolish people, we will learn to be foolish like them. But if we hang around with wise people, we will become wise ourselves.

> "WHOEVER WALKS WITH THE WISE BECOMES WISE, BUT THE COMPANION OF FOOLS WILL SUFFER HARM." (13:20)

The Book of Proverbs tells us a lot about what foolish people are like. Foolish people hate knowledge (1:22; 18:2; 23:9)—they think they know everything already. Foolish people are constantly upsetting their parents (10:1; 15:20; 17:21, 25). They are always talking bad about other people (10:18). Fools think doing evil things is fun (10:23). They are reckless and careless (14:16). They are constantly causing fights (18:6). Fools are always doing the same foolish things—they never seem to learn their lesson (26:11).

Wise friends are very different. They don't get upset when they are corrected or instructed, because they want to learn (9:8; 10:8; 13:1). Wise people run far away from evil (14:16). They make their parents proud (10:1; 15:20). Wise people know when to speak and when to be silent (29:11). They know how to lead others to God (11:30).

Jesus is the best and wisest friend we can have. The Bible says in Him are hidden all the treasures of wisdom (Col. 2:3). The Spirit of God gave Jesus incredible wisdom (Is. 11:2). Every morning His Father woke Him up to teach Him (50:4). Because of this, Jesus always chose the right path. He always rejected evil. He knew exactly what to say and how to say it. Best of all, He calls us His friends, because everything His Father taught Him, He made known to us (John 15:15).

It is important to be friendly to others, but our closest friends should have an attitude of wisdom like Jesus, not the attitude of a fool.

QUICK INTERPRETATION FOR CORRECTION:

This means if we want to become wise and godly people we should hang out with wise people.

DIALOGUE QUESTIONS

1. Would you say your friend is generally pretty wise or foolish?

2. Do you want to become wise? What are the benefits of being wise?

3. Who is the best example of a wise friend? (Jesus)

OTHER PROVERBS

"One who is righteous is a guide to his neighbor, but the way of the wicked leads them astray." (12:26)

"Leave the presence of a fool, for there you do not meet words of knowledge." (14:7)

"Make no friendship with a man given to anger, nor go with a wrathful man, lest you learn his ways and entangle yourself in a snare." (22:24-25)

"Iron sharpens iron, and one man sharpens another." (27:17)

BITTER VS. FORGIVING

BIBLE STUDY:

It is a fact of life that people will offend us. People will sin against us. Even our closest friends and family can hurt our feelings.

The key is how we should re-act when someone sins against us. This proverb says there are two ways we can react. We can either bury the sin, or we can bring it back up over and over.

"WHOEVER COVERS AN OFFENSE SEEKS LOVE, BUT HE WHO REPEATS A MATTER SEPARATES CLOSE FRIENDS." (17:9)

If someone sins against us, we might want to make them feel bad for what they did. So instead of for-giving them, we bring up what they did to us over and over. We might tell other peo-ple what they did to us. This proverb reminds us, if we do that, this will only cause problems. If we don't forgive people, eventually those people won't be our friends anymore.

Instead, we should forgive. Forgiveness means we don't try to get back at them for what they did to us. Even if someone has done something that hurt us, we wish that person well, we pray for them, and we try to be at peace with them. This proverb says if we want to stay friends with someone, we need to "cover" their sins. We leave their sins in the past, and we don't bring them up again.

Jesus knows more about forgiveness than anyone else. He told His disciples we should always forgive those who sin against us. If we don't forgive others, it only shows that we don't really trust Christ's power to forgive us of all our sins (Matt. 6:14-15).

Jesus didn't just tell His disciples to forgive. He did it Himself. Even at the most painful moment of His life when others were nailing Jesus to the cross, Jesus prayed, "Father, forgive them, for they know not what they do" (Luke 23:34). Can you imagine having someone hurt you so badly and still wanting to forgive them? That's how much Jesus loved others. He didn't try to get revenge on anyone.

We need to be the same way. Just as Christ forgives everyone who trusts in Him, we should forgive everyone who sins against us.

QUICK INTERPRETATION FOR CORRECTION:

This means if we want to stay friends with someone, we should always forgive them and not bring up their sins over and over.

DIALOGUE QUESTIONS

1. When you reminded us of how this person sinned against you, was that a forgiving thing to do?

2. Would you want to be friends with someone who was always reminding you of your sins?

3. Did Jesus hold a grudge or try to get revenge on people?

OTHER PROVERBS

"Hatred stirs up strife, but love covers all offenses." (10:12)

"Good sense makes one slow to anger, and it is his glory to overlook an offense." (19:11)

"Do not say, "I will repay evil"; wait for the Lord, and he will deliver you." (20:22)

"Do not say, 'I will do to him as he has done to me; I will pay the man back for what he has done.'" (24:29)

COMPLAINING VS. GRATEFULNESS

BIBLE STUDY:

Do you know our attitude can impact our health? This proverb tells us one of the things that helps us to be healthy is joy. If we are cheerful, it actually helps our bodies. Even modern medicine tells us this. Laughing can relieve tension and pain, increases the flow of blood in our bodies, and even helps our bodies fight disease. But when we are sad, it makes us feel weak, tired, and even increases the risk of getting sick.

"A JOYFUL HEART IS GOOD MEDICINE, BUT A CRUSHED SPIRIT DRIES UP THE BONES." (17:22)

One of the best ways to have joy is to be thankful. The Bible says we should "Rejoice always, pray without ceasing, give thanks in all circumstances" (1 Thess. 5:16-18). No matter the circumstance or situation in our lives, even when things are really bad, we should remember what we are thankful for. This is how we can have joy even when things are not going well.

But what really crushes our spirit is when we complain. When we complain about our circumstances, when we forget what we should be thankful for, we can become sad pretty quickly.

Jesus was a man who was full of joy. The Bible says he was glad when the faith of His disciples grew (John 11:15). He rejoiced knowing His disciples' names were written in heaven (Luke 10:20-21). He felt joy when He obeyed His heavenly Father (John 15:9-11). It was because of "the joy that was set before him" that He was able to endure the cross (Heb. 12:2). Even though the cross was very painful and shameful, He was focused on the joy that would follow: He was focused on His resurrection, getting to be with His Father again, and all the people who would be forgiven because He died for their sins.

He could have complained on the cross. He could have been bitter and mad. But instead, He was joyful, right up to the very end.

We should try to be the same way. When things aren't going our way, instead of complaining, we should focus on what we are thankful for.

QUICK INTERPRETATION FOR CORRECTION:

This means joy makes us feel great, but when our hearts are sad, it makes us feel terrible.

DIALOGUE QUESTIONS

1. Are you focusing only on what you want or are you thankful for what you have?

2. How does complaining make you feel?

3. Was Jesus a complainer or was He joyful?

OTHER PROVERBS

"Anxiety in a man's heart weighs him down, but a good word makes him glad." (12:25)

"The fear of the Lord leads to life, and whoever has it rests satisfied; he will not be visited by harm." (19:23)

"Sheol and Abaddon are never satisfied, and never satisfied are the eyes of man." (27:20)

MAKE A LIST OF PRESSING BEHAVIORAL ISSUES YOUR CHILD STRUGGLES WITH.

_____

_____

_____

_____

_____

_____

_____

_____

_____

_____

_____

PICK THE TOP 2 OR 3 BEHAVIORS YOUR CHILD
NEEDS TO WORK ON. PICK A PROVERB FOR
EACH ISSUE. WRITE THE PROVERB ON THE
LINES NEXT TO THE ISSUE.

MEMORY CARDS

Download an 8.5x11 copy of the memory verse flashcards at

http://www.intoxicatedonlife.com/proverbs-flashcards/

The password to open the file is

parenting

**Features a total of 80 memory verse flashcards
in the following topics:**

Prideful vs. Humble

Complaining vs. Gratefulness

Bitter vs. Forgiving

Bad Friendships vs. Good
Relationships

Quarreling vs. Peacemaking

Envious
vs. Rejoicing with Others

Hurtful Words vs. Kind Words

Argumentative vs. Obedient

Indifferent
vs. Attentative to Elders

Greedy vs. Generous

Emotionally Impulsive
vs. Self-controlled

Deceitful vs. Truthful

Sloppy vs. Diligent

Lazy vs. Hard-working

Made in the USA
Lexington, KY
12 June 2018